EXPLORING THE BEAUTY OF AMERICA

EXPLORING THE BEAUTY OF AMERICA

HANLEY STANLEY

CONTENTS

1 Chapter 1: Introduction to RV Road Trips   1

2 Chapter 2: Planning Your RV Adventure   5

3 Chapter 3: Pacific Coast Highway: The Ultimate Coa   9

4 Chapter 4: Route 66: The Iconic Cross-Country Adve
13

5 Chapter 5: The Great River Road: Following the Mis   17

6 Chapter 6: Alaska Highway: The Last Frontier Exped   21

7 Chapter 7: Conclusion and Final Tips   25

Copyright © 2025 by Hanley Stanley
All rights reserved. No part of this book may be reproduced in any manner whatsoever without written permission except in the case of brief quotations embodied in critical articles and reviews.
First Printing, 2025

CHAPTER 1

Chapter 1: Introduction to RV Road Trips

RV Road Trips: Your Ultimate Adventure

Embarking on an RV road trip is the perfect combination of comfort and freedom. Imagine the vast panoramas drifting by, the adventures awaiting beyond mountains and beaches, at major festivals and cowboy-sized rodeos, or even back at the RV park. We want you to end your "RV virgin" status with a fantastic road trip packed with national park touring, live music, scenic byway explorations, and country fair-going happiness. That's right; we went all out and planned an epically American RV road trip just for you!

Whether you prefer quirky, kitschy, or authentic down-home vibes, we've got it all. This adventurous route covers plenty of roads and miles, but each destination is worth the journey. After all, isn't location just as important for an RV road trip as the road itself? Boogie through Austin in a unique blend of Texas Country, Irish Folk, and Louisiana blues at the annual Austin City Limits festival. Dance in circles at Zilker Park, where you can catch live performances from greats like Van Morrison, Tom Petty, and the Decemberists.

Benefits of RV Travel

RV travel offers myriad benefits, unparalleled by other forms of travel:

1. **Flexibility and Freedom**: Unlike airplanes, RVs allow you to travel at your own pace. Spot something interesting? Feel free to stop and explore.
2. **Cost-Effective**: Living in an RV eliminates hotel rental costs, making it a budget-friendly option.
3. **Convenience**: With an RV, you have all your essentials in one place, removing the need to book hotels or worry about packing and unpacking.
4. **Closer to Nature**: RV travel immerses you in the great outdoors, making you feel truly connected to nature.
5. **Engage with Local Communities**: RV travelers often seek to engage with local communities, frequenting local restaurants, attractions, and learning about the history of each area. They tend to spend more money in these communities than typical travelers.

Choosing the Right RV

Setting off on a scenic RV road trip can be one of the most affordable and fulfilling ways to travel. Here are some key points to consider when choosing the right RV:

1. **Vehicle Handling**: If you're not a professional driver, select an RV that is easier to maneuver.
2. **Sleeping Space**: Ensure the available sleeping space meets your needs, whether you're traveling solo, with family, or with friends.
3. **Budget Considerations**: The cost can vary significantly from one campervan to another. Choose a vehicle that fits

your budget while offering the necessary convenience and comfort.
4. **Company Reputation**: Select a company that values its customers and maintains its vehicles well. Look at the options provided by different rental companies to find the best fit for your trip.

No matter what type of RV you choose, an unforgettable adventure awaits. Embrace the journey and enjoy every beautiful, diverse part of the forest, from mountains to the open plains.

CHAPTER 2

Chapter 2: Planning Your RV Adventure

Preparation is Key

An RV adventure can indeed be a trip of a lifetime, but preparation is essential. If you're renting an RV, do your homework to select the right vehicle. Which type suits your needs best? For families, a spacious Class C could work wonders, while couples might opt for something more compact and maneuverable. Research rental companies to find one with a stellar reputation for safety checks and customer service. Many companies also provide training for first-time RV drivers.

Make a list of crucial considerations before setting off:

- Route planning: Does the rental company allow one-way rentals if you're not returning to your starting point? Apps like Roadtrippers can be immensely helpful.
- Campsites and RV parks: Research where you will park, how and where to dispose of waste, and where to swap gray and black tanks.
- Emergency Preparedness: Ensure the rental company offers a comprehensive safety check and repair services.

Selecting the Ideal Route

The beauty of RV trips lies in the journey rather than the destination. Reading about other families' RV trips can provide inspiration. While planning your trip, it's critical to decide on a route tailored to your interests. Most RV road trips are about soaking in the experience, not just traveling from point A to B.

Consider these factors when planning your route:

- **Scenic Attractions**: National parks, mountains, beaches, and other natural wonders.
- **Climate**: Be mindful of the weather during your travel dates.
- **Points of Interest**: Roadside attractions, historical sites, and charming small towns.
- **Outdoor Activities**: Opportunities for hiking, biking, fishing, and more.
- **Flexibility**: Plan a route that allows spontaneous detours and stops.

When crafting an itinerary, involve the entire family. Discuss everyone's interests and preferences and include stops that excite each member. A flexible, balanced itinerary can cater to varying tastes, ensuring everyone has a memorable experience.

Essential Packing List

Packing for an RV trip is all about balancing essentials with limited space. Here's a comprehensive checklist to ensure you're well-prepared:

General Essentials:

- Bedding (sheets, pillows, blankets)
- Cookware and dishes (pots, pans, plates, utensils)
- Toiletries and personal care items

- Insect repellent and sunscreen
- First-aid kit

Additional Items for Convenience:

- Food storage containers with tight-fitting lids
- Multi-function tools (e.g., multi-tool with can-opener, knife, pliers)
- Duct tape for quick fixes
- Basic tool kit
- Weather radio
- Cooler for drinks
- Additional storage solutions

Contingency Planning:

- Extra batteries and bulbs for the RV
- Layered clothing for varying temperatures (including wool socks, bucket hat, and warm accessories)
- A well-stocked first-aid kit
- Binoculars for observing wildlife
- Gear for planned activities (biking, hiking, fishing)

Weather Considerations:

- Preparing for different climates (warm blankets, layering shirts, jackets for cool weather)
- Proper footwear (hiking boots, comfortable walking shoes)

Packing strategically ensures you're ready for any scenario or adventure that comes your way. Always prioritize essentials, yet be realistic about space and avoid overpacking. This way, you can focus on enjoying your road trip to the fullest.

CHAPTER 3

Chapter 3: Pacific Coast Highway: The Ultimate Coa

The Magnificent Pacific Northwest

Explore the stunning Pacific Northwest with its snow-capped mountains, lush evergreen forests, and picturesque coastal towns. You'll visit celebrated cities, iconic national parks, awe-inspiring forests, and top-notch zoos. The Pacific Coast Highway (PCH) is one of the most beautiful coastlines in the US, but it doesn't stop at Los Angeles. By the time you travel from Seattle, Washington through to LA's Orange County, you'll cover more than 1,600 miles. Each stop along the way has unique experiences, whether it's the glorious beaches, one-of-a-kind rock formations, or expansive views of the Pacific Ocean.

Highlights:

- **Tongva Park**: Feel the Beverly Hills dirt underfoot.
- **Del Norte Coast Redwoods State Park**: Marvel at the towering redwoods.
- **Harbor of the Rocks**: Watch sea lions at play.

Famed attractions between Seattle and Los Angeles offer a delightful blend of natural and urban experiences:

- **Point Reyes National Seashore**: Soak up the breathtaking coastal views.
- **San Francisco County**: Enjoy the vibrant city life.
- **Big Basin Redwoods State Park**: Wander through ancient forests.

Santa Cruz and Monterey Regions

As you drive south, spend a few days in the Santa Cruz and Monterey regions. These areas are rich in attractions and offer plenty of fun for travelers of all ages:

- **San Francisco Zoo**: Get up close with a diverse range of animals.
- **California Academy of Science**: Dive into the wonders of science and nature.

Santa Cruz boasts farm-to-table dining options, catering to brew fans and wine enthusiasts. The county's orchards are filled with a variety of fruits and nuts. Alternatively, depart from Napa to explore the beach cities and tranquil vistas along Highway 1.

Picnic Spots:

- **Between Hermosa Beach and Morro Bay**: Perfect for a scenic lunch break.
- **Conn Valley**: Enjoy the tranquil beauty on your journey to Santa Barbara.

Starting Point: Seattle, Washington

For those ready to invest the time and energy, an RV adventure spanning over 2,000 miles offers indescribable beauty and memorable experiences. While the Washington coast's scenic wonders are a treat, our journey starts in Seattle. This city, known for its high-tech industry and Starbucks' birthplace, hosts a wealth of history and cultural diversity. From famous attractions like Pike Place Market to decadent dining at Dahlia Lounge and El Gaucho, the city offers thrills for everyone.

Must-Sees in Seattle:

- **Space Needle**: Iconic views of the city.
- **Ye Olde Curiosity Shop**: Fun for all ages.
- **Port Townsend**: A ride on a historic whaling schooner.

Leaving Seattle, head south on I-5 through Tacoma to the capital city of Olympia. Consider taking U.S. 101 to embrace the visual extravaganza of the Olympic Mountains. This 3-night, 4-day adventure offers a sensory delight from Seattle to San Francisco, California.

Key Stops Along the Way

Taking your time to soak in the sights is paramount on this road trip. The Pacific Coast Highway is famous for its scenic beauty, making it a road tripper's dream.

Key Stops:

- **Pfeiffer Beach, Big Sur**: Walk along the stunning coastline.
- **Shrine Drive-Thru Tree, Myers Flat**: Drive through a massive redwood.
- **Colorful Garden of Nurseries, Eureka**: Ogle the vibrant flowers.

With over 426 miles of road trip-worthy sights, this journey is a feast for the eyes. Stretching along 655 sun-soaked miles, the PCH takes travelers from Los Angeles' sunshine and beaches to the bohemian delights of San Francisco. Drive through Big Sur's cliffs, explore vibrant towns steeped in surf culture, and witness the majestic forests of redwoods.

A Taste of the Route:

- **Beverly Hills**: Glamour and beaches.
- **Santa Cruz**: Countryside charms.
- **San Francisco**: Coastal and urban blend.

This journey promises sunsets to remember, offering a mini-vacation away from California's bustling cities. Experience the unique natural beauty of the United States along every mile of the Pacific Coast Highway.

CHAPTER 4

Chapter 4: Route 66: The Iconic Cross-Country Adve

A **Journey Through Time**
America's Mother Road, Route 66, is synonymous with adventure, dreams, and the spirit of exploration. This historic highway stretches across 2,400 miles from Chicago, Illinois, to Los Angeles, California. Though decommissioned in 1985, Route 66 remains a beloved journey for RV adventurers, offering a path through time and Americana culture.

Throughout your journey, you'll encounter quirky attractions and classic Americana, from Spanish-influenced architecture and neon signs to vintage diners and motels. Unique stops include prohibition-era drinking spots, military museums, and larger-than-life statues. Oklahoma boasts the longest drivable stretch of the Mother Road—a must-see is Buck Atom's Cosmic Curios On 66 featuring murals and a towering 21-foot statue.

Historical Significance
Route 66 holds a special place in American history and culture. Often referred to as the "Main Street of America," it symbolized hope during the Dust Bowl and Great Depression as thousands ven-

tured west towards California in search of a better life. Gas stations, diners, and motor courts sprung up along the highway, creating economic lifelines for small towns. Over the years, Route 66 evolved into a scenic tourist route, capturing the hearts of summer vacationers and leisure travelers.

By the 1930s, Route 66 had become an icon of American culture, frequently mentioned in songs, TV shows, and radio broadcasts. It witnessed high-speed police chases, military movement during World War II, and countless travelers embarking on new beginnings. The National Park Service notes how travelers were treated to grand parades and festivities upon reaching California.

Route 66's glory days were characterized by bustling roadside attractions and colorful characters, from neon-lit motels to lively towns filled with intrigue and charm. Small-town festivals, like Missouri's annual "The Last Person to Leave" event, showcased the camaraderie and resilience of communities along the route.

Must-See Attractions

Route 66 is renowned for its unique and diverse attractions, making it an ideal adventure for road trip enthusiasts. Here are some must-see stops:

- **Cadillac Ranch (Amarillo, Texas)**: A legendary landmark featuring ten colorfully painted Cadillacs buried nose-first into the Texas prairie.
- **The World's Largest Rocking Chair (Cuba, Missouri)**: This giant rocker provides a perfect photo op, delighting visitors with its whimsical charm.
- **The World's Largest Catsup Bottle (Collinsville, Illinois)**: A 170-foot water tower shaped like a bottle of ketchup, a beloved roadside attraction.

- **Gatekeeper on the Hill (Catoosa, Oklahoma)**: Sporting a ten-gallon hat and eyepatch, this figure was built to attract travelers to a filling station and diner.
- **Quapaw Bridge (Quapaw, Oklahoma)**: Known as the "Bridge to Nowhere," this suspension bridge offers a unique photo opportunity.
- **Tri-State Marker**: Stand at the point where Kansas, Missouri, and Oklahoma meet, and soak in the crossroads of three states.
- **Casinos of Joplin, Missouri**: Take a gamble and enjoy the lively entertainment at these iconic establishments.

Tips for Traveling Route 66

Traveling Route 66 requires careful planning to make the most of your adventure:

1. **Seasonal Considerations**: Some attractions are seasonal, so plan your trip accordingly.
2. **Route Maps**: Utilize resources like the Illinois Route 66 Scenic Byway website for detailed road maps and historical sites.
3. **Engage with Locals**: RVers on Route 66 often share great advice on quirky stops and hidden gems. Engage with fellow travelers for tips.
4. **Emergency Preparedness**: Keep a well-stocked emergency kit and ensure your vehicle is in good condition.

By blending historical significance with modern-day attractions, Route 66 offers an unforgettable cross-country experience. Embrace the journey, immerse yourself in the culture and history, and create lasting memories on America's most iconic highway.

CHAPTER 5

Chapter 5: The Great River Road: Following the Mis

Scenic Highlights

The Great River Road is a stunning driving route that spans state and US highways, including Interstate 90 and U.S. Route 61. As you travel along this picturesque journey, you'll encounter the ever-changing Mississippi River – from breathtakingly beautiful landscapes to historical marvels, environmental challenges, and serene oases.

The Great River Road follows the Mississippi River from its headwaters in northern Minnesota to the Gulf of Mexico, covering around 3,000 miles. This route is marked and maintained by the governments of ten states: Minnesota, Wisconsin, Iowa, Illinois, Missouri, Kentucky, Tennessee, Arkansas, Mississippi, and Louisiana. Traveling from north to south on the west bank of the river from St. Louis to the Gulf offers a unique adventure.

Notable Scenic Spots:

- **The Driftless Region**: Known for its evasion from glacial movement, this area boasts captivating landscapes, romantic rail-trails, and dramatic caves.
- **Bald Eagle Observations**: Between Wabasha and Red Wing, Minnesota, you'll witness flocks of wintering Bald Eagles.
- **Confluence of Rivers**: At Prescott, Minnesota, the American, St. Croix, and Black Rivers converge with the mighty Mississippi, creating rattling eddies.
- **Prairie du Chien**: Adventure seekers will enjoy the stunning views from steel-frame overlooks and wooded cliff-dimensions, particularly at Wyalusing State Park.
- **Fort Piatt Historical Park**: Located on U.S. 61 between New Boston and Gladstone in Illinois, this park offers some of the most beautiful golden sunrises.

Throughout the route, designated overlooks and parks offer unobstructed views of classic, unaltered waterfronts. Travelers can soak in the beauty of sinuous bluffs, rising farmlands, and dense natural woodlands.

Cultural Experiences

The Great River Road is not only a journey through captivating landscapes but also a rich cultural tapestry. This route flows through areas filled with cultural diversity, festivals, and events, earning recognition in National Geographic Traveler's list of Drives of a Lifetime.

Not-to-Miss Cultural Experiences:

- **Amish Settlements**: Discover the unique lifestyle and traditions of Amish communities along the route.
- **Bettendorf's Riverboat Casino**: Try your luck at this iconic riverside attraction.

- **National Mississippi River Museum and Aquarium**: Located in Dubuque, Iowa, this museum offers an immersive experience into the natural and cultural history of the river.
- **Dickeyville Grotto**: Explore quirky concrete creations in Dickeyville, Wisconsin.
- **Large Cities and Small Towns**: From the cosmopolitan vibes of Minneapolis and St. Louis to the charm of small river towns, there's something for everyone.
- **Smithsonian-Affiliated Museums**: Visit riverside museums in St. Cloud, Minnesota, and beyond for a dose of history and culture.
- **Trail of Tears**: Learn about this historic route and its significance in American history.
- **Blues Music**: Enjoy the rhythm and soul of blues music up and down the river.

The Great River Road offers an array of historical experiences, from ancient mounds and bluffs to adobe forts and steamboat baronial museums. The stories of the people, their artifacts, and the architecture showcase the unique cultural tapestry that makes this journey one for the books.

CHAPTER 6

Chapter 6: Alaska Highway: The Last Frontier Exped

Alaska Highway's Legendary Path

One of the greatest charms of RV travel is the freedom of the open road, allowing for spontaneous exploration. The Alaska Highway, also known as the Alcan Highway, offers an unforgettable journey through British Columbia, the Yukon, and the heart of Alaska. Loaded with stunning panoramas, including a mountainous road built right through the Rockies, this expedition presents the raw soul and wilderness of the dwindling Last Frontier. It's less of a road trip and more of a pilgrimage.

Historical Significance

Alaska Highway's history is full of legends, roughnecks, and remarkable stories. Built during World War II, this road was essential in protecting North America's west coast. Nearly 11,000 men and tons of equipment were mobilized to construct the highway between 1939 and 1943, at an immense cost of around $150 million. The road officially opened to the public on October 25, 1942, and many of the camping sites and boondocking berths exist today, giving travelers a sense of history while they explore.

Diverse Wildlife Encounters

Traversing the Alaska Highway offers some of North America's most diverse wildlife encounters. You'll encounter four types of bears: black bears, grizzly bears, brown bears, and the elusive polar bears, found much farther north. Moose are plentiful, especially in the Yukon Territory's southern areas. Away from towns and campsites, you may spot elk, caribou, and dall sheep high on the cliffs. Eagles are a common sight in the skies, adding to the majesty of the journey.

As you venture farther north into Alaska, the opportunities to spot wildlife continue to grow:

- **Wrangell-St. Elias National Park**: Look out for large bull moose drawn by mineral-rich grounds.
- **Kennecott and Wonder Lake**: Moose and caribou sightings abound in these mineral-rich areas.
- **Dalton Highway (Haul Road)**: Traveling north of the Arctic Circle, this route offers bountiful wildlife viewing, including caribou and moose.

Remote Camping Spots

For those who dislike urban camping's hustle and bustle, the Alaska Highway offers a variety of remote camping spots where nature reigns supreme. These spots provide breathtaking views and pure, entrancing beauty. The magnificent Top of the World Highway, for example, features vistas often above the tree line, offering a close connection with nature.

Notable Remote Camping Sites:

- **Muskeg Lake Campsites**: Enjoy stunning views of snow-covered mountains and turquoise shadows reflected in the

lake's waters. The unparalleled serenity of these remote sites makes them perfect for a peaceful getaway.
- **Remote Arcane Lakes and Mountains**: Discover hidden spots where hissing squirrels and squabbling camp robber-jays dominate the quiet forests. These sites offer both lake and mountain vistas, providing an ideal backdrop for a meditative camping experience.

Each morning at these sites, you'll be greeted by clear skies, sunshine on snow-covered peaks, and the boundless beauty of untouched wilderness. Every day spent on this journey creates memories that will be etched in your mind forever.

The Alaska Highway journey is more than just a road trip—it's an adventure into the raw, untamed beauty of one of the last true frontiers on Earth.

CHAPTER 7

Chapter 7: Conclusion and Final Tips

In conclusion, embarking on an RV road trip across America is an adventure like no other. From selecting the optimal RV for your group to budgeting the trip and plotting your route, from setting up the RV to engaging with the wilderness, this journey is filled with learning, discovery, and unforgettable moments.

Despite encountering some challenging weather, the trip was a resounding success. The stunning wildlife, serene landscapes, and invigorating hikes created lasting memories. Esther not only learned how to cook inside the RV but also mastered plotting stops and campsites on RV Trip Wizard. She discovered that driving an RV off-road can be quite the thrilling adventure. The trip also exposed her to diverse accents and even autotune—a social experiment in itself.

Key Takeaways

1. **Embrace the Journey**: This RV adventure ignited a passion for road trips and a desire to travel more—not just around America but the entire world. The journey revealed a new degree of beauty and brightness beyond the grey cityscapes.

2. **Learn and Adapt**: Flexibility is crucial. Esther's newfound cooking skills and knack for navigating helped make the trip smoother and more enjoyable.
3. **Connect with Nature and Culture**: Engaging with the wilderness and absorbing the cultural richness of different regions added depth and meaning to the journey.

Final Tips for Future RV Trips

1. **Check the Weather**: Before setting off, review the weather forecast. Consider driving in the evening if rain is predicted during the day, ensuring you have daylight for hiking and exploring.
2. **Secure Funds**: Ensure you have enough cash for your security deposit by using drive-through or drive-up ATMs near your RV pick-up spot.
3. **Plan for Reversing**: If towing a vehicle, having a spotter for your first trip can be immensely helpful, especially when reversing.

This adventure across America's diverse landscapes fostered a love for the open road, ignited curiosity for new destinations, and created memories to cherish for a lifetime. As you plan future RV trips, remember to embrace the journey, learn from each experience, and connect with the beauty and culture of the places you visit.

www.ingramcontent.com/pod-product-compliance
Lightning Source LLC
LaVergne TN
LVHW092102060526
838201LV00047B/1532